Brilliant Blunders & Fortunate Flops

101 Random Facts, Funny Mistakes, and Stories of Inventions That Changed the World by Accident! A Fun Science & History Book for Curious Kids Ages 7-107!

By T. J. Harvey

Contents

Introduction

Some inventions are carefully planned. Others... trip over a dog, fall into a pile of mould, and discover antibiotics.

This book is packed with 101 accidental discoveries that shaped the world – from snacks and science to sticky notes and silly toys. Every story is real, slightly ridiculous, and surprisingly world-changing.

So flip the page, have a laugh, and remember: sometimes the best ideas start with a mistake.

Psst... Don't miss the bonus "Did You Know?" fun facts hiding at the end of the book – even more awesomeness awaits!

101 Accidents That Changed the World

1. Penicillin Power: Alexander Fleming's Mouldy Petri Dish (1928)

In 1928, Alexander Fleming returned from vacation to find his lab in a delightful state of chaos. One Petri dish had gone mouldy (ew), but instead of throwing it out, he noticed something weird: the bacteria around the mould were totally wiped out. The mould didn't just grow – it *fought back*.

That mould was **Penicillium notatum**, and Fleming had just discovered **penicillin**, the first true antibiotic. It took a few more scientists and some years to develop it into medicine, but eventually, it became a bacteria-busting hero, saving millions of lives.

And to think, it all started because he didn't clean up before going on holiday. The next time someone nags you about tidying your room, just say you're *doing science*.

2. Teflon: Slippery Science for Sticky Situations (1938)

Roy Plunkett wasn't trying to revolutionise breakfast. He was just messing around with gases to create better refrigerants. But one day, one of his pressurised gas canisters stopped working. When he opened it, he found it was coated with a smooth, waxy white powder that didn't stick to anything.

That powder? It became **Teflon** – a super slippery material that resists heat, chemicals, and everything else. Originally used for military and industrial applications, it later became the champion of **non-stick frying pans**, stain-resistant fabrics, and even **space suits**.

It wasn't made for cooking, but it changed kitchens forever. Scrambled eggs slid around like figure skaters.

So yes – thanks to a random chemical hiccup, your pancakes don't cling to the pan, your spaghetti doesn't glue itself to the pot, and astronauts don't come home covered in moon dust. Nice one, Roy.

3. X-Rays: Seeing Through Stuff (1895)

Wilhelm Röntgen was fiddling with cathode rays (aka weird glowing tubes) when he noticed something strange. His screen started glowing... even though there was a thick object in the way. He tested it using his wife's hand and – creepy alert -he could see her bones on a photographic plate.

He had discovered invisible energy beams that could pass through soft tissue but not bone. Since he had no idea what they were, he called them **X-rays**, because "X" means "mystery." His wife called them "terrifying." (Fair.)

Suddenly, doctors could see inside bodies without cutting them open. Broken bones, swallowed coins, mysterious chest lumps – X-rays became the superhero of medical tools.

From spooky glow to lifesaving scan, this accident lit up the world (and your skeleton).

4. Dynamite: Ka-Boom Courtesy of the Lab (1867)

Alfred Nobel was fascinated by **nitroglycerin** – a liquid that could blow up just about anything. Great for construction. Also great for unplanned explosions. One day, some of the volatile liquid spilled on a pile of sawdust. But nothing happened. Strange!

He realised the sawdust had **absorbed** the nitroglycerin, making it way less likely to go BOOM at the wrong time. That led to the creation of **dynamite**, which could be shaped into sticks, stored safely, and used to blast tunnels, build railroads, and make mining faster (and slightly less terrifying).

But Nobel felt uneasy. He didn't want to be remembered just for explosives. So, he left his fortune to create the **Nobel Prizes**, including one for peace.

Kaboom, with a side of conscience

5. Popsicles: A Chilly Mistake (1905)

Frank Epperson was 11 when he accidentally made history. One cold night in 1905, he left a cup of homemade soda outside with a stir stick in it. The next morning- -t had frozen solid. Instead of crying about his ruined drink, he pulled it out by the stick and licked it.

Boom: frozen juice on a stick. He named it the "Epsicle," but his kids (many years later!) thought that sounded weird. They called it a **Popsicle**, and honestly, they were right.

Years later, he patented the invention, and it became a favourite summer snack around the world. Cherry, grape, orange, or mystery blue – they all owe their existence to a forgetful kid and a chilly night.

Who says accidents can't be tasty?

6. Velcro: Burrs and a Brilliant Brain (1941)

George de Mestral was just a guy on a hike with his dog. When they got home, the dog was absolutely covered in burrs. You know the type, those little round clingy balls that stick to everything like nature's glitter. Most people would've groaned and reached for a comb. George grabbed a microscope.

What he saw amazed him: the burrs were covered in tiny **hooks** that clung to **loops** in fabric and fur. And that's when inspiration struck, what if he made a fastener that worked the same way?

After years of tinkering, **Velcro** was born. It was a hit with NASA (for space suits), kids' shoes, and people who hate zippers. All thanks to one stubborn hike, one hairy dog, and a curious mind.

Stick with it – it might just change the world.

7. Coca-Cola: Fizz That Started as Medicine (1886)

Dr. John Pemberton was trying to invent a miracle medicine. He mixed up a syrup made from coca leaves and kola nuts – hence the name – and hoped it would cure headaches and give people a little pep. But when a batch accidentally got mixed with fizzy water, something unexpected happened.

It didn't just taste okay. It tasted *amazing*.

He started selling it at pharmacies as a tonic. People loved the taste more than the health claims, and Coca-Cola quickly fizzed its way out of the medicine cabinet and into vending machines, sports stadiums, and backyard BBQs.

So yes, what started as a medicinal mishap became the world's most famous soft drink. No prescription required, just ice and a smile.

8. Super Glue: Sticky Stuff That Wouldn't Let Go (1942)

During World War II, chemist Harry Coover was trying to invent a material for clear plastic gun sights. Instead, he made a substance that was way too sticky. It bonded instantly to everything – glass, metal, fingers, you name it.

Totally unusable for weapons. Totally annoying in the lab. So he shelved it.

Years later, while working on jet canopies, his team stumbled across the same formula again. One lab accident (and some very stuck equipment) reminded them of its power. This time, they saw the potential, and Super Glue was born.

It became a household hero: fixing broken mugs, busted toys, and anything cracked in a moment of panic.

From military flop to miracle fix-it-in-a-flash, Super Glue proves that sticking with your mistakes might just pay off.

9. Saccharin: Accidental Sweet Tooth (1879)

Constantin Fahlberg, a chemist, was elbow-deep in coal tar experiments (because that's how all sweet stories begin). After a long day in the lab, he went home for dinner, without washing his hands. Gross, right?

But then… his food tasted sweet. He hadn't added sugar. It was his fingers!

He ran back to the lab, retraced his steps, and discovered **saccharin**, the world's first artificial sweetener. Sweet enough to launch a sugar-free revolution, all thanks to coal gunk and poor hygiene.

The moral? Wash your hands. Unless you're trying to invent diet soda.

10. Microwave Oven: Zapped Snack Attack (1945)

Percy Spencer was working with radar equipment when he noticed something strange: a chocolate bar in his pocket had melted. Weird. So he tried popcorn next. It popped. Then an egg – it exploded (messy, but promising).

Percy had accidentally discovered that **microwaves** could cook food. He refined the process, and soon the first microwave ovens were born – though the originals were the size of a fridge and cost as much as a car.

Luckily, they got smaller and cheaper. Today, we zap popcorn, pizza, soup, and midnight snacks with the press of a button.

All thanks to a melty chocolate bar, an exploding egg and a radar engineer with snacks. Delicious progress!

11. Potato Chips: Cranky Chef's Crunchy Revenge (1853)

It all started with a very picky diner. At a fancy restaurant in Saratoga Springs, a customer kept sending back his fried potatoes, saying they were too thick and soggy. The chef, George Crum, was not amused. So, to teach the guy a lesson, he sliced the potatoes paper-thin, fried them until they were crunchy, and dumped on way too much salt.

Revenge snack? Yes. Total fail? Nope.

The customer loved them, and soon everyone wanted the new crispy treat. Crum's little act of culinary sass became a hit, and before long, **potato chips** were everywhere.

Today, we munch billions of them every year, at barbecues, picnics, and straight from the bag at midnight. All thanks to one angry chef and a guy who wouldn't stop complaining.

12. Silly Putty: Bouncy Blob from a Boring War (1943)

During World War II, rubber was in short supply, and scientists were scrambling to invent a substitute. James Wright, an engineer at General Electric, mixed boric acid with silicone oil and voilà! – he created a strange, gooey blob that stretched, bounced, and lifted ink off newspapers.

Useful for tyres? Not even close.

But when someone realised how much fun it was to squish, stretch, and bounce, **Silly Putty** became a toy-store legend. They packaged it in little plastic eggs, gave it a goofy name, and kids everywhere went nuts for it.

From failed war material to wacky desk toy, this pink goop proved that not all heroes wear capes. Some come in an egg and stick to comic strips.

13. Corn Flakes: Breakfast Born of a Blunder (1894)

Dr. John Harvey Kellogg and his brother Will were running a health spa where they served super-bland food. One day, they accidentally left cooked wheat sitting out too long. When they finally remembered it, they tried to roll it out, but it crumbled into thin, flaky pieces instead.

Instead of throwing it away, they toasted the flakes, and to their surprise, it tasted... good!

They named it **Corn Flakes** (after switching from wheat to corn), and Will eventually added sugar to make it taste even better. It became the spark that launched a breakfast empire.

So, if you've ever eaten cereal while still in your pajamas and not totally awake, you can thank two forgetful brothers and a really dry breakfast mistake.

14. Play-Doh: From Wall Cleaner to Doughy Delight (1950s)

Believe it or not, **Play-Doh** started as a cleaning product. In the early 1950s, people used soft, doughy putty to wipe coal soot off wallpaper. But as homes switched to cleaner heating, the wall-wiping business went cold.

One employee noticed something interesting: his kids loved squishing the leftover dough. It was soft, safe, and perfect for rolling into blobs and snakes. So, they added bright colours and a fun name, and boom – **Play-Doh** was born!

It quickly became a hit in schools and homes, where it's still squished, rolled, and smushed to this day. From wall cleaner to creativity booster, this mistake was a true hands-on success.

And bonus – it smells weird but in a comforting way.

15. Velveeta: Gooey Gold from a Cheese Oops (1918)

In a cheese factory in New York, workers had a problem: making Swiss cheese left behind lots of weird scraps and broken bits. Normally, they'd toss them out. But this time, someone had a better idea, melt it all down, smooth it out, and mix it into a creamy new product.

The result was shiny, stretchy, and oddly satisfying. It didn't melt like regular cheese, it oozed. They named it **Velveeta**, and it became the go-to cheese for dips, grilled sandwiches, and anything involving lots of noodles.

Sure, it's not "fancy" cheese – but it's cheesy, meltable, and came from leftovers. Basically, it's the underdog of the dairy world.

16. Inkjet Printers: Coffee Meets Chemistry (1977)

A Canon engineer was enjoying his coffee while working near a hot soldering iron. He absentmindedly touched his pen to the heat... and *splat!* – a tiny blob of ink shot out. Instead of wiping it up, he had a lightbulb moment: what if heat could be used to fire ink onto paper?

He started experimenting, and soon the company developed **thermal inkjet printing**, the technology behind many of today's home and office printers. You've probably used one to print birthday invites, school reports, and photos of your cat in a party hat.

From spilled coffee to high-tech printing, this accidental mess became a quiet revolution. And all thanks to a pen, a hot plate, and maybe a caffeine habit.

17. Cheese Puffs: Factory Fire Turns Tasty (1930s)

At a corn processing plant in Wisconsin, workers were using machines that cooked animal feed under steam pressure. One day, someone noticed that when moistened cornmeal got squeezed through a heated tube, it puffed out like magic.

Naturally, someone tasted it (as you do). It was crunchy and light, and weirdly addictive. They added some seasoning, then cheese flavouring, and boom! **Cheese puffs** were born.

What started as livestock feed became the ultimate snack food. Neon-orange fingers, cheesy grins, and a snack that crunches like a firecracker, thanks to a curious worker and a machine with attitude.

Who knew pig chow could be so delicious?

18. Matchsticks: Explosive Stirring (1826)

In 1826, chemist John Walker was mixing chemicals (probably while humming something scientific) when he accidentally dipped a wooden stick into a compound. Later, as he stirred with it, the tip scraped the table and *whoosh!* – it burst into flame.

Walker had just invented the first **friction match**, and he didn't even mean to. He called them "lucifers" because... well, they made fire. Dramatic? Yes. But also very effective.

Soon, people were carrying fire in their pockets (safely!) for candles, pipes, and campfires. One tiny spark changed everything.

So if you've ever lit a birthday candle without rubbing two sticks together – thank a clumsy chemist and his flammable furniture.

19. LSD: A Wild Ride from Fungus (1938)

In 1938, Swiss chemist Albert Hofmann was studying **ergot fungus**, hoping it might help improve blood circulation. After handling one compound, he felt... *odd.* Dizzy. Dreamy. Extremely trippy.

He had accidentally absorbed **LSD** through his fingertips.

Days later, curious about the effects, he took a small dose on purpose, and rode his bicycle home while experiencing wild hallucinations. That day is still known as "Bicycle Day" by fans of psychedelic science.

Though controversial, LSD opened up new areas of research in psychology and brain science. It also launched some *very* interesting album covers.

From mushroom mould to mind-blowing mistake, this one was a trip – literally.

20. Plastic: The Prize That Changed Everything (1907)

Inventor Leo Baekeland was trying to create a better electrical insulator. What he ended up with was **Bakelite**, the first fully synthetic plastic. It could be shaped, heated, cooled, and reused. Basically, it was like playdough for grownups, but tougher and a lot more useful.

At first, it was used in things like telephone casings and electrical parts. Then came buttons, radios, toys, jewellry – plastic was everywhere.

Baekeland had accidentally opened the door to a whole new era. From Tupperware to toothbrushes, this slippery invention changed how we store, seal, wear, and *clutter* our homes.

Oops... and also, wow.

21. Safety Glass: A Crash That Didn't Shatter (1903)

French chemist Édouard Bénédictus was working in his lab when he accidentally dropped a glass flask. It fell to the floor and... didn't shatter! It cracked but stayed in one piece. Curious, he inspected it and realised the flask had contained a plastic solution that dried inside, creating a film that held the glass together.

Most of us would say, "Huh, weird," and move on. But Bénédictus saw potential. He developed **laminated safety glass**, layers of glass with a thin plastic sheet in between – that doesn't explode into shards.

Now it's everywhere: in car windshields, phone screens, and even your fish tank. Thanks to one clumsy chemist and a surprisingly safe crash, we can take a few bumps without the drama of a thousand tiny shards flying everywhere.

Breaking things isn't always a bad thing. Especially in a lab coat.

22. Post-it Notes: Sticky That Wasn't Sticky Enough (1968)

At 3M, Dr. Spencer Silver was working on a super-powerful glue. What he made instead was... disappointing. It was barely sticky. It held paper, but only lightly, and peeled off with no mess. No one knew what to do with it.

Then his coworker Art Fry had a forehead-slap idea. He sang in a church choir and kept losing his place in the hymn book. Regular bookmarks slid out. But what if he used that weak glue to make notes that could stick – just a little – and then come off cleanly?

Thus, **Post-it Notes** were born. Bright, handy, movable reminders now stick to fridges, monitors, maths books, and brains across the world.

All because one glue wasn't sticky enough, and a singer needed to keep his place. Sometimes, being a little clingy works out perfectly.

23. Scotchgard: Couch Saver from a Sneaky Spill (1952)

Patsy Sherman was a chemist trying to make rubber coatings for jet fuel hoses. One day, a few drops of a test formula splashed onto her lab assistant's white canvas shoes. Instead of leaving a stain, the liquid *bounced off*. No water, oil, or dirt could penetrate it.

Most people would've wiped it off. But Patsy saw a golden opportunity. She ran more tests and refined the formula into **Scotchgard**, a stain-resistant coating now used on furniture, carpets, backpacks, and raincoats everywhere.

So next time you spill spaghetti sauce on the couch and it wipes right off, raise a glass (carefully) to Patsy and a pair of spotless sneakers.

Some of the greatest inventions start with, "Oops... wait a minute."

24. Slinky: Springy Stair Dancer from a Shipyard Goof (1943)

Engineer Richard James was working on tension springs to stabilise naval equipment. One day, he dropped a coil and watched it tumble... but instead of plopping down like a rock, it flipped end over end, gliding across the floor like it had a mind of its own.

Mesmerised, he took it home. His wife Betty saw the toy potential and gave it a name: **Slinky**. Within a year, it was selling out in stores. Kids were captivated by the way it "walked" down stairs, jiggled on tables, and tied itself in impossible knots.

From military equipment to toy box legend, the Slinky has been bouncing around the world for over 75 years.

Proof that a perfect fall can be a perfect invention.

25. Anaesthesia: Party Trick Turned Surgical Revolution (1840s)

In the 1840s, a new craze swept through town: **laughing gas parties**. People would inhale nitrous oxide, burst into giggles, and stumble around numb and goofy. It was the TikTok challenge of the Victorian era.

Dentist Horace Wells attended one of these events and saw someone hurt themselves – but they didn't feel a thing. A lightbulb went off: what if this stuff could make surgery painless?

He began testing it on dental patients, and it worked. Soon, other doctors joined in, and **anaesthesia** changed the face of medicine. Literally. Now surgeries involve dreams, not screams.

So yes, thanks to some silly partygoers and a dentist with curiosity, we don't have to bite down on sticks while getting a tooth pulled.

26. Levi's Jeans: Gold Rush + Ripped Pants (1873)

During the California Gold Rush, miners had two major problems: not finding gold... and their pants kept falling apart. Canvas tents were tough, pants were not. Enter Levi Strauss, a dry goods seller, and tailor Jacob Davis. Together, they created trousers reinforced with rivets and made from tough fabric.

The result? Jeans. Sturdy, rugged, and ready to survive anything from digging ditches to dancing in saloons.

Originally sold to miners, cowboys, and railroad workers, **Levi's jeans** eventually became a fashion statement. Movie stars wore them. Rockstars wore them. Even presidents wore them. (Probably not while panning for gold.)

From ripped trousers to global wardrobe staple, all thanks to a mining mishap and a guy who knew his fabrics.

27. Ice Cream Cones: A Crunchy Coincidence (1904)

At the 1904 St. Louis World's Fair, an ice cream vendor ran out of bowls just as crowds lined up for a treat. He panicked, no bowls meant no scoops! But nearby, a Syrian waffle maker named Ernest Hamwi was selling thin, crisp pastries.

Thinking fast, Hamwi rolled one into a cone and handed it to the ice cream guy. The frozen scoop nestled perfectly into the crispy pastry, and the crowd went wild.

Soon, other vendors copied the idea, and the **ice cream cone** became a permanent summer staple. Cold, creamy, and now completely portable.

Who knew dessert history could be made by a waffle and a moment of panic?

28. Quinine: Bitter Medicine Becomes a Classic Drink (1800s)

Back in the 1800s, British soldiers in malaria-prone India were told to drink **quinine** to keep the disease at bay. The problem? Quinine was extremely bitter – like chewing a battery. So they tried mixing it with soda water, sugar, and lime to make it tolerable.

The result was **tonic water**. Add a splash of gin (optional – for adults only), and the now-famous **gin and tonic** was born.

Originally a mosquito-fighting remedy, it became a bubbly beverage with a medical excuse. (Doctors probably wouldn't recommend it *now*, but it sounded convincing at the time.)

Thanks to a bitter gulp and a creative mix, the tonic water we sip today has a history that's anything but dry.

29. Stainless Steel: A Rusty Problem Solved by Accident (1913)

Harry Brearley was trying to create a more durable gun barrel. He experimented by adding chromium to steel, but the test samples were tossed aside as failures. Weeks later, someone noticed those discarded pieces hadn't rusted, even after being left in the open.

Brearley had accidentally created **stainless steel**, a shiny, rust-resistant metal that wouldn't corrode or stain easily. It quickly found uses far beyond gun barrels: kitchen sinks, cutlery, elevators, medical tools, skyscrapers, you name it.

All because someone checked the scrap pile.

It's a reminder that even failures deserve a second look – and that sometimes, the leftovers shine the brightest.

30. Bubble Wrap: From Wallpaper Fail to Shipping Win (1957)

In 1957, engineers Alfred Fielding and Marc Chavannes were trying to invent 3D textured **wallpaper**. The idea? Airy, futuristic-looking walls made of plastic with little bubbles inside. Sounds cool, right?   It flopped. No one wanted lumpy plastic on their walls.

But the bubbly plastic had one unexpected superpower: it was amazing at protecting fragile stuff. So they rebranded it as **Bubble Wrap**, and soon it became the go-to packaging material for shipping electronics, glassware, and – bonus! – for anyone who loves popping bubbles just for fun.

Now it's famous for keeping packages safe and being *incredibly satisfying to pop*. From décor disaster to shipping superstar. Because when life gives you weird wallpaper, make it go *pop*.

31. Cheese: Spoiled Milk Makes It Big (Ancient Times)

Thousands of years ago, someone, probably a very sweaty goat herder, poured milk into a pouch made from an animal stomach. Hours later, when they opened it, surprise! The milk had curdled into solids and liquids: curds and whey. Instead of gagging and tossing it, someone *tasted* the weird chunks. Boom – **cheese** was born.

It turns out that enzymes in the stomach lining, mixed with warm weather and bumpy travel, naturally transformed milk. Different conditions led to different types – soft, hard, stinky, sharp. Today, we have thousands of varieties.

From mozzarella on pizza to cheddar in lunchboxes, cheese owes its existence to bad milk, a long walk, and someone very brave with no lactose intolerance.

It might've started as an accident, but it aged into perfection. Like, well... cheese.

32. Plastic Wrap: Lab Spill That Stuck Around (1933)

At Dow Chemical, a researcher was experimenting with dry-cleaning gases when one canister turned into a surprise: it had formed a thin, clingy film inside. Curious, he poked at it and discovered it stuck to *everything* – hands, shelves, paper, noses.

Originally, it was used in the military to protect aircraft parts from moisture and dirt. But when someone wrapped it around a sandwich, they realised it was also perfect for keeping food fresh.

Enter **plastic wrap** – aka cling film, aka the thing you can never pull off the roll without rage.

A lab mishap made it stick around in kitchens and cafeterias forever. Proof that even sticky accidents can be deliciously useful.

33. WD-40: Rocket Science Goes Off-Label (1953)

A team of engineers at Rocket Chemical Company (yes, that was really the name) was trying to invent a formula that stopped rocket parts from rusting. After 39 failed tries, formula #40 finally worked. It **displaced water** perfectly, so they called it **WD-40**.

The product worked so well, the scientists started taking it home to fix squeaky doors, sticky bike chains, and jammed locks. Eventually, the company gave in and sold it to the public.

It was never meant for household chores – but now, it's a tool-shed legend.

From outer space to your garage shelf, WD-40 is a slippery superstar with a numerical name. Not bad for formula number 40.

34. The Credit Card: Restaurant Embarrassment to Financial Empire (1949)

Frank McNamara was out to dinner when he realised he had forgotten his wallet. Big oops. His wife had to bail him out, and Frank was *mortified*. Determined to avoid future humiliation, he thought: "What if you could pay later, with a card?"

He developed the **Diners Club Card**, the first widely accepted credit card. At first, it only worked at restaurants, but it grew fast, soon shops, airlines, and gas stations got on board.

Today, credit cards are everywhere, from contactless taps to online checkout buttons.

So if you've ever bought something with a swipe, a beep, or a click, you owe it all to a very awkward dinner.

35. Corn Dogs: Deep-Fried Discovery at the Fair (1920s-1940s)

Corn dogs may not sound like science, but their creation is a true food experiment. In the early 20th century, vendors at state fairs were looking for fast, hand-held meals. Someone got clever: take a hot dog, coat it in cornbread batter, and deep-fry it on a stick.

The idea may have emerged in Texas or Illinois (no one's quite sure), but the result was instant magic: crispy on the outside, savoury on the inside, and perfect for walking and eating at the same time.

What began as a portable lunch became a fairground icon. No plates, no forks, just one glorious golden stick of joy.

All hail the **corn dog**, born of batter, oil, and pure carnival chaos.

36. Cellophane: Clear Wrap from a Wine Spill (1908)

Swiss chemist Jacques Brandenberger wanted to invent a fabric that wouldn't stain. After watching someone spill wine on a tablecloth, he figured: let's make something totally liquid-proof.

He tried coating cloth with a see-through plastic, but the plastic peeled off in one shiny, crinkly sheet. It didn't make fabric better, but it was *really good* on its own. So he scrapped the cloth idea and focused on the film.

That shiny film became **cellophane** – perfect for wrapping food, flowers, and anything that looks better when you can *see it* first.

From soggy linens to snack display star, this invention proves that spilled wine isn't always a disaster. Sometimes, it's just the beginning of something beautifully clear.

37. Instant Photography: Film That Was Too Fast (1947)

Edwin Land was taking photos of his daughter on vacation when she asked the question that changed photography: "Why can't I see the picture *now*?"

At the time, all photos had to be developed in a lab. But Land couldn't stop thinking about her question. Back in his lab, he experimented with layered film that developed the photo internally, instantly.

Soon, the **Polaroid camera** was born. Snap the picture, wait a few seconds, and *voilà!*, your goofy face, blurry pet, or half-eaten sandwich appeared like magic.

What started as a child's question became a photo revolution. Instant memories, zero patience required.

38. The Stethoscope: Shyness Sparks a Sound Solution (1816)

French doctor René Laennec felt awkward putting his ear directly on a woman's chest to listen to her heartbeat. So instead, he rolled up a piece of paper into a tube, and was amazed at how much clearer the sound was.

From that humble paper cone, he developed the **stethoscope**, giving doctors a simple way to listen to hearts and lungs without ear-to-chest awkwardness.

Today's versions are fancier, but the idea is the same – listening closely, from a polite distance.

From shyness came science. And now we all get to hear the *lub-dub* loud and clear.

39. Tea Bags: A Steeping Slip-Up (1908)

In 1908, tea merchant Thomas Sullivan wanted to send tea samples to customers. Instead of using tins, he packaged small portions in silk pouches to save money. But his customers got confused, they dunked the whole bag into hot water.

And they loved it.

Without meaning to, Sullivan had invented the **tea bag**. Later versions switched to gauze and paper, but the idea stayed the same: mess-free, no-strainer-required tea.

Today, tea bags dominate the market, letting people steep with ease at home, at work, or while pretending to be fancy.

From silk sample to global staple, this invention proves that confusion plus boiling water = convenience.

40. Vaseline: Oil Rig Gunk Goes Glam (1859)

In 1859, workers on Pennsylvania oil rigs noticed something odd, sticky black goo kept clogging up their machinery. Annoying, right? But they also noticed that when they rubbed it on small cuts or burns, they healed faster.

A young chemist named Robert Chesebrough got curious. He refined the goo into a smooth, clear jelly and tested it on himself (including minor burns). It worked!

He named it **Vaseline** and marketed it as a miracle skin salve. People used it for everything – chapped lips, dry skin, diaper rash, even squeaky hinges.

From sticky oil gunk to bathroom essential, Vaseline proves that even the grossest goo can go glam.

41. Rubber Vulcanisation: A Stormy Surprise (1839)

Charles Goodyear was obsessed with rubber. The problem? It melted in heat, cracked in cold, and stuck to everything. Basically, it was terrible.

One winter day, in a mix of frustration and science rage, he accidentally dropped a rubber-and-sulfur mix onto a hot stove. When it cooled, something incredible had happened, the rubber was tougher, stretchier, and weather-resistant!

He'd stumbled upon vulcanisation, the process that makes rubber useful. Now it's in tyres, shoes, sports balls, and bouncy-house castles.

Goodyear was broke most of his life, but he gave the world bouncy soles and durable wheels. So if you've ever bounced, rolled, or driven anywhere, thank the man who literally cooked up rubber.

42. Oobleck: Slime Science from a Children's Book (1949)

A curious teacher was reading Dr. Seuss's *Bartholomew and the Oobleck* – a book about sticky green goo falling from the sky – and decided to make some for fun. By mixing cornstarch and water, they got a strange substance that acted like a liquid *and* a solid.

Punch it? It's hard. Slowly poke it? It oozes. Totally bizarre.

This experiment turned into the now-famous classroom favourite: Oobleck. It's used to teach kids about non-Newtonian fluids, substances that don't follow the usual rules of liquids.

From a silly book to science lesson slime, Oobleck is the only goop that makes your brain hurt and your hands happy.

Just don't eat it. Dr. Seuss never said it was soup.

43. Pacemaker: A Heartfelt Malfunction (1956)

Engineer Wilson Greatbatch was building a device to record heart rhythms when he accidentally installed the *wrong* resistor. Instead of just recording a beat, the circuit gave off rhythmic electrical pulses.

Wait... pulses? Like... a heartbeat?

He realised it could help people with irregular heart rhythms. That mistake led to the invention of the implantable pacemaker, a life-saving device now used by millions around the world.

From an oops on the workbench to a heartbeat helper, this is one mistake we're *very* glad happened.

Sometimes the wrong part makes everything work just right.

44. Safety Pins: Fidgeting Pays Off (1849)

Walter Hunt was an inventor with a habit of tinkering, and debts. Lots of debts. While nervously twisting a bit of brass wire, he bent it into a coil and sharpened one end... then folded the other end into a clasp to protect delicate fingers.

Boom – the safety pin was born.

It was small, cheap to make, and incredibly useful. He sold the rights for $400 to pay off a bill (oops), but his invention stuck around forever.

Now they're in sewing kits, baby drawers, punk rock fashion, and emergency costume repairs everywhere.

All thanks to a fidgety guy and a springy bit of wire. Not bad for a moment of productive anxiety.

45. Coloured Glass: A Medieval Mistake with Style (Ancient & Middle Ages)

Early glassmakers were melting sand and soda ash when they noticed impurities, like iron, copper, or gold, sometimes turned the glass different colours. At first, it seemed like a flaw.

But those "mistakes" were beautiful.

By the Middle Ages, artists had mastered the technique, using minerals to colour glass and creating incredible stained glass windows for churches and cathedrals. They used gold for red, cobalt for blue, and even ashes for green. Who knew impurities could be so pretty?

What started as bad chemistry became glowing works of art that told stories with sunlight.

So next time you see coloured glass, remember: sometimes the best beauty comes from being a little bit... imperfect.

46. Synthetic Dye: Purple Fashion from a Failed Cure (1856)

Teenage chemist William Perkin was trying to make synthetic quinine to cure malaria. Instead, he cooked up a dark, gunky mess in his lab. Not exactly life-saving medicine.

But when he cleaned his beaker, he noticed the residue turned a brilliant purple. Intrigued, he dabbed some on fabric, and it *stuck*. Brightly. Permanently. Beautifully.

He had accidentally created the world's first synthetic dye, later called mauveine.

At the time, purple was rare and expensive, worn mostly by royalty. Perkin's accidental dye made it affordable and fashionable. It sparked a colour craze across Europe and kickstarted the modern chemical industry.

From failed medicine to purple power, William's mistake painted the world a little brighter.

47. The Lava Lamp: Psychedelic Science in a Cocktail Shaker (1963)

British inventor Edward Craven Walker spotted a bubbling egg timer made from wax and liquid inside a cocktail shaker at a pub. It wasn't very useful, but it was mesmerising.

He tinkered with the formula, using wax, oil, and coloured water, and put it in a tall glass tube with a lightbulb underneath. The heat melted the wax into slow, hypnotic blobs. He called it the **Astro Lamp**, but we now know it as the **lava lamp**.

It became an icon of the 1960s and 70s, decorating dorm rooms, discos, and groovy bachelor pads everywhere.

Not bad for something that started out as a glorified egg timer.

48. Silly String: Serious Chemistry, Goofy Result (1972)

Chemists Leonard Fish and Robert Cox were developing a sprayable plastic for use in medical casts, something that could wrap quickly and harden into shape.

What came out of the test can, though, was a stringy, squiggly, springy mess that *definitely* wouldn't support a broken arm – but it was really fun to shoot across the room.

So instead of a cast-maker, they created a party toy. **Silly String** was born!

Today, it's used at birthday parties, parades, weddings (maybe not yours), and even by soldiers to detect tripwires. From medical prototype to toy-store staple, Silly String is one big colourful whoops.

49. Smart Dust: Tech That Fell Off a Truck (1990s)

While developing micro sensors for battlefield surveillance, researchers accidentally dropped a few off a table. The tiny particles scattered and still worked – transmitting data wirelessly from the floor.

Oops... or genius?

The team realised they had created smart dust: teeny-tiny sensors that could monitor everything from temperature to movement, all while being nearly invisible.

Today, smart dust is used in environmental science, factories, and even space missions. It's still evolving, but the idea began with a dropped prototype and a very surprised engineer.

From high-tech tumble to microscopic marvel, smart dust proves that when stuff breaks, breakthroughs sometimes follow.

50. Instant Noodles: Solving Hunger with a Fryer (1958)

After World War II, Japan faced food shortages, and ramen was hard to get. Momofuku Ando wanted to create a fast, affordable meal. He tried everything – boiling, drying, baking – until one day, he flash-fried noodles in oil.

They became dry, shelf-stable, and could be rehydrated in hot water in minutes. Instant noodles were born!

He launched them as "Chikin Ramen" in 1958. Later came the cup version, which added boiling water straight to the package.

From hunger solution to dorm-room legend, instant noodles are the edible MVP of lazy lunches and midnight snacks.

All thanks to one fryer, a food shortage, and a man who really loved ramen.

51. Nylon: A Fibre Born from a Chemical Fiddle (1935)

Wallace Carothers was playing with polymers at DuPont, trying to create a super-strong synthetic fibre. One day, he pulled a gooey strand from a beaker, and it stretched without snapping. Weird, but promising.

That goo became **nylon**: the world's first fully synthetic fabric.

Originally used for toothbrush bristles, it quickly moved to **stockings**, **parachutes**, and **ropes**, especially during WWII, when silk was scarce. Soon it was in everything from jackets to guitar strings.

It all started with a scientist tugging on sticky spaghetti in a lab. Sometimes, stretchy messes are just fashion waiting to happen.

52. Popsicle Rocket Fail Becomes Fireworks Classic (Early 1900s)

A fireworks maker was testing tiny cardboard rocket tubes when one misfired, flew into the air, and spun wildly with a *pop-pop-pop*.

It didn't go high, but it looked amazing. He added colour powder, reworked the design, and soon the **Roman candle** was born, later evolving into the "popping peony" fireworks we see today.

Accidental fizz became festival magic.

So the next time you're watching a firework fizzle, crackle, and explode, remember: it might have started as a dud that forgot to go straight.

53. Braille: A Cannonball-Sized Problem Solved (1820s)

In the French army, soldiers were supposed to read night time orders using a "night writing" system, raised dots to feel in the dark. But the code was clunky and hard to learn.

One young boy named Louis Braille, who had been blinded in a childhood accident with a **cobbler's awl**, thought he could do better. He simplified the code into six-dot cells that were easier to read by touch.

At just 15, Louis had created the system now known as **Braille**.

He didn't invent it on purpose – he just wanted books blind people could actually read. And now, millions can.

From one painful accident came a whole new way to read the world.

54. Dry Cleaning: A Greasy Coincidence (1840s)

A French tailor named Jean Baptiste Jolly noticed his tablecloth got cleaner after his maid spilled lamp oil on it. Instead of yelling, he leaned in for science.

Turns out, the kerosene dissolved greasy stains better than water.

Jolly experimented and opened one of the first **dry cleaning businesses**, using solvents instead of soap and water to clean delicate clothes. It wasn't exactly eco-friendly (early solvents were a bit... explosive), but the idea stuck.

Now, thanks to a clumsy spill and a curious tailor, you can rescue your best suit from salad dressing disasters.

55. Bubblegum: Blown by a Lab Assistant (1928)

Walter Diemer, an accountant at a chewing gum factory, liked to tinker with gum formulas in his spare time. One day, he mixed a batch that was stretchier and less sticky than usual. He gave it a try... and it **blew a bubble**.

No one else had pulled that off. Ever.

The company dyed it pink (the only food colouring on hand), and **bubblegum** hit the shelves. It sold out in a day. Kids couldn't get enough of blowing bubbles, popping them, and then getting it stuck in their own eyebrows.

From office hobby to mouth party, this invention proves that even accountants can cause chewing chaos.

56. Windshield Wipers: Rainy-Day Flash of Genius (1903)

Mary Anderson was riding a streetcar in New York during a rainy day when she noticed the driver had to keep stopping to wipe the windshield by hand. That meant slow rides, grumpy passengers, and soggy sleeves.

When she got home, she sketched out a swinging blade powered by a lever inside the vehicle – something drivers could operate without leaving their seats.

People thought it was silly at first, "Who needs wipers? Just stick your head out the window!" But by the 1920s, windshield wipers were standard on most cars.

Mary's rainy ride inspired a safety feature we now totally take for granted. Next time it pours and your wipers save the day, remember: it all started with one frustrated woman and a foggy front window.

57. Rice Krispies Treats: Snap, Crackle... Surprise! (1939)

Kellogg's employees Malitta Jensen and Mildred Day were tasked with creating a fundraiser snack using **Rice Krispies** cereal. They melted marshmallows and butter, stirred in the cereal, and pressed it into a pan.

Boom – **Rice Krispies Treats** were born.

They weren't trying to invent a dessert. They were just trying to sell cereal and help out the local Girl Scouts. But people went bonkers for the gooey, crunchy squares, and the recipe was printed on cereal boxes soon after.

Now, it's a classic snack for bake sales, birthdays, and late-night pantry raids.

Sometimes, sweet success is just three ingredients and a lucky stir away.

58. Velcro Sneakers for Kids: Tiny Hands, Big Idea (1950s)

Velcro had already been invented for space suits and outdoor gear, but it wasn't until someone realised kids couldn't tie their laces that the magic truly clicked.

A shoe company tested **Velcro fasteners on sneakers**, and suddenly bam! – every kid could put on their own shoes without help, tantrums, or knots the size of a hamster.

It wasn't the original intention, but it became one of Velcro's biggest wins. Parents rejoiced. Teachers cheered. Shoelaces sobbed quietly in the corner.

Sometimes, the best inventions aren't brand new – they just find the perfect use.

59. Coloured Pencils: An Artist's Oops (1800s)

Early artists used graphite sticks for sketching, but sometimes they'd grind pigments and press them into soft leads to add colour. One day, a pencil maker accidentally mixed in wax while processing pigments, and the colour stuck to paper *better*.

It blended. It shaded. It didn't smudge like chalk. This mistake gave birth to the modern **coloured pencil**.

Artists and kids alike loved the smooth texture and vibrant colours. Schools and studios never looked back.

From messy pigments to perfect pencils, this happy accident brightened up everything from notebooks to masterpieces.

60. Microwave Popcorn: Snack + Science Combo (1981)

Microwaves had been around since the 1940s, but **microwave popcorn** didn't pop onto the scene until someone noticed how great the appliance was for making kernels explode in fluffy joy.

Engineers figured out how to seal kernels and buttery flavour inside a heat-sensitive pouch. When microwaved, the pouch inflated, the corn popped, and your living room smelled like a cinema.

It was faster, cleaner, and way less flammable than stovetop methods.

From lab lunch to lazy movie night MVP, microwave popcorn is one small bag for snacks, one giant leap for couch potatoes.

61. Slurpee: A Brain Freeze Born from a Broken Machine (1950s)

At a Dairy Queen in Kansas, Omar Knedlik's soda machine broke down. So, he stuck some bottles in the freezer to keep them cold. When customers opened them, the soda was **slushy** and half-frozen – and they loved it.

Omar realised he was onto something and built a machine that could *intentionally* freeze and fizz soda into a sweet, slushy treat.

He called it the **ICEE**, and when 7-Eleven licensed it, they renamed it the **Slurpee**, a name inspired by the sound you make slurping it down too fast (and getting a brain freeze).

From freezer fail to frozen fame, Slurpees turned summer into a slurpable science.

62. Speed Bumps: A Bumpy Way to Slow Down (1906)

Engineer Arthur Holly Compton was sick of cars zooming through his neighbourhood. He needed a way to slow them down without yelling "SLOW DOWN" every five minutes.

So he tested an idea: a raised bump in the road. Cars that drove over it too fast got a nasty jolt. Instant lesson learned.

The first **speed bump** wasn't meant to be global, but it worked so well that cities everywhere started copying the idea.

Today, speed bumps save lives, protect neighbourhoods, and launch unsuspecting coffee cups into orbit. All thanks to a guy who turned road rage into roadside genius.

63. The Etch A Sketch: Electric Trick Turns into Toy (1950s)

French inventor André Cassagnes was installing a light switch cover when he noticed that pencil marks he made on a plastic sheet **showed up on the other side**. Static electricity had pulled the particles into place.

Intrigued, he built a box with aluminum powder inside and a stylus that moved behind the screen using knobs. Drawings appeared... and could be erased with a shake.

Voila: the **Etch A Sketch** was born!

It became one of the most iconic toys of the 20th century. Kids everywhere mastered stair-step houses, wobbly spirals, and unintentional blobs. Some even got good at it (unicorn-level rare).

All because of static cling and a curious electrician.

64. Daylight Saving Time: A Nap-Lover's Dream? (1895)

New Zealand entomologist George Vernon Hudson wanted more daylight after work to study bugs. So, he suggested moving the clocks forward in summer.

Around the same time, British builder William Willett also proposed the idea, he hated wasting daylight while people were still sleeping.

Eventually, countries adopted **Daylight Saving Time** during wartime to save fuel. The idea stuck (even if no one really understands why we still do it).

From bug-hunting to bunkers, this clock-shifting scheme came from two guys who just wanted more time in the sun.

And now we're all confused twice a year. Thanks, science!

65. Safety Elevator: Falling Platforms Prompt Genius (1852)

Early elevators were scary. If the rope snapped, *down you went* – and not in a good way.

Enter Elisha Otis, who invented a **safety brake** that would catch the elevator if the rope broke. To prove it worked, he stepped into a platform at a public expo and ordered the rope cut. Everyone gasped... and the elevator *stopped* safely.

The crowd went wild. Otis's elevator became standard in buildings, making skyscrapers possible and staircases avoidable.

From daredevil stunt to city skyline changer, his "fall-proof" idea lifted us all to new heights.

66. Gatorade: Sweaty Football Players Made Science (1965)

A coach at the University of Florida asked doctors why his football players were collapsing in the heat. The answer? They were sweating out fluids and salts faster than they could replace them.

So, scientists whipped up a drink to replenish electrolytes and water. It tasted awful, but it worked. The team's performance soared, and they started winning. The drink? Named after the team: the **Florida Gators**. Gator + Aid = **Gatorade**.

Eventually, they added flavours people could actually swallow, and it became the drink of athletes, gym rats, and anyone with a cold.

All thanks to football, Florida heat, and very sweaty science.

67. Glow Sticks: Accidental Party Chemistry (1960s)

Scientists were experimenting with chemicals that reacted to light. One day, someone mixed hydrogen peroxide with a fluorescent dye and a special activator in a sealed plastic tube.

It **glowed**. Brightly. Without heat or electricity. Oops?

This chemiluminescent reaction was meant for emergency lighting and military use, but someone realised it was perfect for *parties*.

Glow sticks made their way into concerts, raves, parades, and Halloween bags worldwide. Snap, shake, and shine.

From serious science to dance-floor accessory, these glowing tubes turned chemistry into a celebration.

68. Fingerprinting: Greasy Prints on a Slide (1880)

Dr. Henry Faulds was studying ancient pottery in Japan when he noticed something weird – **fingerprints** preserved in the clay. Each one was different. Later, after catching a lab assistant with suspicious inky fingers on a glass slide, he realised fingerprints could be used to identify people.

He wrote to scientists (including Charles Darwin!) saying fingerprints were unique and permanent. Eventually, police forces around the world adopted them as a way to catch criminals.

A greasy smudge turned into one of the most important tools in forensics.

Next time you unlock your phone with a fingerprint, remember: it started with mucky fingers on a microscope slide.

69. Quicksand Myth Busted by Accident (1930s)

Quicksand was once thought to be inescapable, you'd sink and vanish like a cartoon villain. Then in the 1930s, geologists studying swamps stepped in some and... didn't disappear.

Turns out, **quicksand is denser than the human body**. You can get stuck, but you won't sink entirely.

One researcher got caught in it during fieldwork and had to wiggle free with help. It took forever, but no one vanished.

This accidental lesson helped bust myths and create safety guidelines for swamps and construction sites.

Sorry movies – real quicksand just isn't that dramatic.

70. Sticky Notes for Pets: The World's First Pet Message Tag (1990s)

A vet tech in Ohio accidentally discovered that Post-it Notes stuck really well to dog fur – briefly. During a hectic day, she wrote "needs meds" on a note and placed it on a sleepy golden retriever.

The dog trotted off. The note stayed on.

She laughed, but it sparked a trend: quick-labelling pets in clinics before they went to different stations. Soon, she modified the idea using safe, velcro-style tags and lightweight clips.

This happy accident helped improve communication in veterinary clinics around the world.

Just don't try it with cats. Trust us.

71. Colour-Changing Moods: The Mood Ring Mix-Up (1975)

Two inventors, Josh Reynolds and Maris Ambats, were experimenting with **liquid crystal** technology, substances that change colour based on temperature. They were trying to make medical devices that measured body heat... but the crystals were too inconsistent for science.

Still, the colour changes were beautiful and fun.

So they stuck the crystals in a ring and claimed it reflected your *mood* (even though it really just measured finger warmth). Boom **the mood ring** craze was born!

Blue for chill, green for meh, black for drama. Science? Sort of. Fun? Absolutely.

Sometimes feelings *do* come in colours – especially if your fingers are sweaty.

72. Doppler Radar: A Weather Forecast from a War Tool (1950s)

Doppler radar was originally developed for tracking enemy planes. But after WWII, scientists noticed something strange: the radar was also picking up patterns from **storm clouds**.

Meteorologists realised they could use Doppler to track **rain, hail, and tornadoes**, using how the radar signal bounced off moisture in the air. They refined the tech, and soon, weather forecasting took a massive leap forward.

What started as a military spy tool became the go-to system for predicting if you should bring an umbrella or cancel the barbecue.

So yes, the thing that spots incoming doom now helps you plan your outfit.

73. Nerf Balls: Soft Foam, Hard Luck Saved (1969)

Parker Brothers was looking for a new indoor toy. Inventor Reyn Guyer had a foam game idea, but when testers started **throwing the foam balls** around the office, they realised something: they were soft enough to toss *anywhere* without breaking stuff.

Goodbye board game. Hello **Nerf ball**.

It was marketed as the "world's first indoor ball." No lamps shattered. No windows cracked. No noses broken (usually). Kids loved it – and so did parents.

From serious game to squishy chaos, Nerf became a foam empire. Balls, darts, blasters, and that one foam sword every sibling regretfully owned.

74. Chewing Gum: A Sticky Obsession (1860s)

People have chewed tree sap for centuries, but modern **chewing gum** came from an inventor named Thomas Adams. He was trying to turn **chicle** (a tree sap from Central America) into rubber.

Spoiler: it didn't work.

So instead of tyres, he added sugar and mint… and invented something way more fun to chew.

His "Adams' New York Chewing Gum" became a hit. Soon, gum was everywhere: in classrooms, under desks, and occasionally on shoes.

From rubber fail to bubble success, chewing gum proved that you don't need to change the world – just give it something fun to chew on.

75. Ice Cubes in Bottles: Lazy Error to Cool Convenience (1980s)

A soda bottling plant once had a freezer malfunction. The machine that was supposed to chill the bottles just **froze them instead**. They were about to toss the batch – until someone cracked one open and took a sip.

It was icy. It was fizzy. It was amazing.

The frozen soda slush became so popular that it inspired **freezer-friendly bottles** and the "ice-your-drink-in-the-bottle" idea that now appears on sports drinks and sodas everywhere.

From overchilled mistake to marketing trend, this happy accident made cold even cooler.

And yes, brain freeze was part of the deal.

76. PlayStation: A Console Born from Betrayal (1994)

Sony once teamed up with Nintendo to create a CD-based gaming system. But right before the big reveal, Nintendo ditched Sony and partnered with another company. Ouch.

Instead of giving up, Sony took the tech they'd built and developed their own console: the **PlayStation**.

What started as a *revenge project* became a gaming legend. With sleek discs, 3D graphics, and now-iconic games, the PlayStation outsold nearly everyone and changed the industry.

Sometimes heartbreak leads to high scores – and really good boss battles.

77. Pavlov's Dogs: Bell-Ringing Brains and Drool (1890s)

Russian scientist Ivan Pavlov was studying dog digestion when he noticed something odd: the dogs started drooling **before** food arrived, just from seeing lab assistants walk in.

Intrigued, he ran experiments where he rang a bell before feeding them. Soon, the dogs began drooling at the sound alone.

He had accidentally discovered **classical conditioning**, a key idea in psychology.

His plan was to study stomachs, not teach dogs to respond to doorbells. But he changed science forever by noticing slobber.

From snacks to science, it turns out even dogs can teach us a thing or two about learning.

78. Bubble Tea: A Tea Shop's Sweet Stunt (1980s)

In Taiwan, a teahouse owner decided to liven up her cold tea. She added **sweet tapioca pearls**, inspired by chewy dessert balls from street markets. Customers were confused... then hooked.

The drink became known as **bubble tea** – not because of the pearls, but because of the foam from shaking the tea.

It spread from Taiwan to trendy cafes worldwide, with flavours like taro, brown sugar, and "what-is-that?" jelly.

From playful experiment to global sip-sensation, bubble tea proves that drinks are better when they chew back.

79. Toasted Ravioli: A Deep-Fried Dinner Mistake (1940s)

At a restaurant in St Louis's Italian neighbourhood, a busy chef accidentally **dropped raw ravioli into a deep fryer** instead of a pot of boiling water. Instead of panicking (or telling the manager), he fished out the crispy pasta, dusted it with cheese, served it with marinara... and braced for disaster.

But customers loved it.

The crispy outside, gooey inside, and tangy dip turned this kitchen whoops into a crowd-pleasing new dish: **toasted ravioli**. Despite the name, it's deep-fried (not toasted) and it became a local favourite almost overnight.

Now it's a must-have in St. Louis restaurants and game-day menus everywhere. One fryer fumble gave the world pasta that crunches.

Lesson: if you make a mistake in the kitchen, just add cheese and act confident.

80. Garage Door Opener: Spy Tech Hits Suburbia (1950s)

During WWII, engineers created a system to remotely detonate bombs using radio signals. After the war, one clever inventor thought: "What if this opened my garage?"

Using a similar signal system, he created the first **remote-controlled garage door opener**, no more hopping out in the rain to lift heavy doors.

Soon, garages everywhere were going up and down at the push of a button.

From secret missions to suburban convenience, this spy-tech-turned-timesaver is proof that some military leftovers belong in the driveway.

81. Velcro Wallets: From Astronauts to Teenagers (1970s)

Velcro was originally designed for **astronaut suits** and mountaineering gear, practical, rugged stuff. But in the 1970s, someone had a totally different idea: put it in a **wallet**.

The result? The now-iconic **Velcro wallet**, lightweight, nearly indestructible, and loud enough to startle a cat when opened. Teenagers loved the *rriiiipp!* sound, and it became a symbol of cool in playgrounds and skate parks everywhere.

They were colourful, full of zippered pouches, and made kids feel like secret agents managing five bucks and three bubble gum wrappers.

Velcro was never supposed to become fashion, but it *stuck* – literally and culturally.

From space missions to lunch money holders, the Velcro wallet is proof that the best gear isn't always high-tech... just really satisfying to open.

82. Lollipops: Sticky Fingers Lead the Way (1908)

Candy maker George Smith wanted to make hard candy more portable. The problem? Melty, sticky hands.

So he stuck a piece of hard candy on the end of a stick and called it the **Lollipop**, naming it after a racehorse (seriously).

The idea wasn't totally new (people had been putting sweets on sticks for centuries) but George made it catchy, mass-produced, and way easier to eat on the go.

Now lollipops are dentist nightmares and kid party staples everywhere. From root beer to rainbow swirl, they all started with one sticky-fingered idea and a horse with a fun name.

83. Pencil Erasers: Oops! Now You See It, Now You Don't (1770)

Before erasers, people used bread to rub out pencil marks. (Yes – actual squishy bread!) Then one day, English engineer Edward Nairne grabbed a small piece of rubber by mistake instead of breadcrumbs and discovered… it worked better. *Way* better.

He'd accidentally invented the first **rubber eraser**.

At the time, rubber was called "India gum," and it was expensive and weird. But Nairne started selling it, and the name "rubber" stuck – because it rubbed out writing!

Eventually, someone added the eraser to the end of a pencil, saving generations of test-takers and doodlers from permanent regret.

From toast crumbs to classroom saviour, the eraser proves that sometimes the best mistakes are the ones you can wipe away.

84. Earmuffs: Cold Ears, Hot Invention (1873)

Chester Greenwood was just 15 when he decided he'd had enough of freezing ears during winter in Maine. Scarves weren't cutting it. So he asked his grandma to sew **fur circles onto a wire frame** he could wear over his head.

Boom: **earmuffs**.

His friends wanted some. Then his town. Then the U.S. Army, which used them during cold-weather training.

He patented his invention, built a factory, and turned his frosty frustration into a warm business success.

Earmuffs: proof that teenage discomfort is a powerful force for innovation.

85. Paper Towels: A Roll of Accidents (1907)

The Scott Paper Company accidentally produced a massive batch of toilet paper that was too thick and stiff. Totally unusable for its original purpose, but instead of trashing it, someone had an idea.

Cut it into sheets and market it as a **sanitary disposable towel**.

Hospitals loved it. So did schools. Eventually, people started using them at home too. The idea of one-use, germ-free clean-up caught on, and **paper towels** became a kitchen essential.

So next time you spill juice or wipe a peanut-buttery face, thank a roll of rejected toilet paper that found a new purpose.

86. Silly Bandz: Office Supply Meets Animal Kingdom (2002)

A Japanese designer created stretchy silicone bands in fun shapes to use as **eco-friendly rubber bands**. They were meant for office workers who wanted their paperclips to have personality.

But when kids discovered them, it sparked a craze. The bands (now called **Silly Bandz**) came in the shapes of animals, stars, food, and even dinosaurs. They snapped back into shape after being stretched, and soon kids were trading them like candy.

From cubicles to classrooms, a boring office supply became a wrist-hugging fad that bounced through playgrounds around the world.

All because someone thought rubber bands could be... a little sillier.

87. Gravity (Confirmed by a Falling Apple): A Snack-Sized Theory (1600s)

Legend says Isaac Newton was chilling under a tree when an **apple bonked him on the head**. Did he cry? Nope. He thought, "Why did that fall *down* and not sideways or up?"

This led him to study motion, leading to his theory of **gravity** – a force pulling objects toward the Earth's center. He didn't invent gravity (spoiler: it was already working), but he explained how it works.

That apple didn't just fall – it sparked one of the biggest breakthroughs in science.

So yes, sometimes a snack to the skull really *can* be a lightbulb moment.

88. Matchbox Cars: Big Toy Idea, Tiny Accident (1953)

A dad working for a die-cast toy company wanted to impress his daughter, but her school only allowed toys small enough to fit inside a **matchbox**.

So he designed a mini car that *did*. She showed her friends, they wanted one too – and just like that, **Matchbox Cars** were born.

Soon there were fire trucks, hot rods, construction vehicles, and more. All perfectly pocket-sized.

From a school rule to a tiny toy empire, these little cars proved that small things can go vroom in a big way.

89. Snapchat: Self-Destructing Pics by Mistake (2011)

A group of Stanford students were working on a photo-sharing app when one of them asked, "What if the photos **disappeared after a few seconds?**"

The idea was meant as a joke, but it stuck. They built an app where pictures and videos vanished after being viewed. Kids loved it. So did people who hated awkward selfies.

They called it **Snapchat**, and it quickly became one of the world's most-used social media apps.

From silly suggestion to smartphone staple, this disappearing act made history... then vanished 10 seconds later.

90. The Barcode: Lines That Changed Everything (1949)

While sitting on a beach eating ice cream, graduate student Norman Joseph Woodland drew a series of lines in the sand – Morse code, stretched out into thick and thin stripes. He'd been trying to solve a problem: how to scan product information instantly.

That sandy doodle led to the first barcode.

The early machines were clunky, but by the 1970s, barcode scanners were finally fast enough. The first product ever scanned? A pack of chewing gum.

Now, barcodes are everywhere, on cereal boxes, concert tickets, luggage tags, and even hospital bracelets.

From a beach brainstorm to a worldwide beep-fest, the barcode was an idea that really scanned.

91. Frisbee: Pie Tin That Took Flight (1940s)

College students used to toss empty pie tins from the Frisbie Pie Company back and forth for fun. The tins were light, flew surprisingly well, and, if you weren't careful, could knock someone's sandwich clean off the table.

Years later, toy makers saw the fun and designed a plastic version called the Pluto Platter, which was later renamed the Frisbee (a nod to those pie-tossing pioneers).

From dessert plate to disc golf legend, the Frisbee became a backyard staple, a dog's best friend, and the reason your cousin broke that lamp.

Proof that dessert sometimes leads to airborne adventure.

92. Coin Toss: Settling Debates Since Forever (Ancient Rome)

Long before sports refs used it, the coin toss was a decision-making tool in Ancient Rome. Called "navia aut caput" (ship or head), it used a coin with a ship on one side and a head on the other.

People used it to settle arguments, pick leaders, and even decide guilt or innocence in court (yikes).

It wasn't *invented* as a game – it was a serious way to make fate-based decisions when people couldn't agree.

Now it decides football kickoffs, chore duty, and who has to call Grandma.

From high-stakes courtroom to rock-paper-scissors rival, flipping a coin remains the world's most dramatic *plonk*.

93. Yoga Pants: Space Suits to Stretchy Suits (1990s)

Textile engineers were working on new stretchy, breathable fabrics for spacesuits and athletic wear. What they didn't expect? The material would become a fashion explosion.

Originally meant for Olympic athletes and astronauts, the fabric was light, comfy, and durable, perfect for exercise. But then people started wearing it for grocery shopping. And naps. And coffee runs. Suddenly, yoga pants weren't just for yoga.

The athleisure trend was born from accidental comfort and a dash of "Why wear jeans if I don't have to?"

Thanks to space-age materials and chill vibes, stretchy pants took over the planet.

94. Lunchables: A Marketing Shortcut That Worked (1988)

In the late 1980s, Oscar Mayer was struggling to sell bologna. Meat wasn't "cool," and lunch prep was a pain for busy parents.

So their marketing team invented a convenient fix: stackable lunch trays with crackers, cheese, meat, and later, dessert. The team even modelled the packaging after adult TV dinners so kids felt "grown up."

Thus, Lunchables were born: fast, fun, and weirdly satisfying (especially the mini pizzas).

They didn't set out to create an iconic kids' meal – just to save a struggling cold cut.

From meat mess to school lunch hero, Lunchables prove that a little marketing and a lot of crackers go a long way.

95. The Whoopee Cushion: Royal Prank Gone Wild (1920s)

Employees at a rubber factory were playing with leftover sheets of latex when someone sat on a folded one and it made a ridiculous noise. Naturally, they laughed like hyenas.

They brought it to a gag store, and soon, the Whoopee Cushion became a prankster's favourite tool.

Rumour has it they first offered it to a young novelty company, who said it was "too rude." (They later changed their minds.)

From factory floor accident to birthday party essential, the Whoopee Cushion is living proof that fart jokes are forever.

And hey, at least it wasn't real.

96. The Ejection Seat: A Popped Hat That Saved Lives (1940s)

Engineers designing high-speed aircraft needed a way for pilots to escape quickly. Inspiration struck when someone watched a hatch blow off a test plane during a failed takeoff, launching the pilot's helmet into the air.

That spark led to the ejection seat, designed with explosive charges to shoot pilots clear of crashing planes. It was scary, dramatic, and absolutely necessary.

Ejection seats have since saved thousands of lives. They're like a backup plan with fireworks.

From hat-launching mishap to airborne lifeline, this invention proves sometimes the best ideas start with "Oops, where'd that go?"

97. Sneakers: Squeaky Shoes That Took Off (Early 1900s)

Originally, shoes had hard soles that clomped with every step, *not* ideal for sneaking around. But when manufacturers started using rubber for sporting footwear, people noticed something funny: they were almost silent.

That made them perfect for tennis, running, and sneaky children.

The nickname "sneakers" caught on fast, coined by someone who realised these soft-soled shoes made it easier to sneak up on people (and possibly steal cake before dinner).

From court shoes to fashion must-haves, sneakers now rule gyms, catwalks, and school hallways everywhere.

So yes, your favourite kicks started as quiet creepers. Which, when you think about it, makes gym class feel *way* more mysterious.

98. Pavement Striping: Paint Spill Saves Lives (1911)

While driving behind a milk truck that dripped white liquid, Dr. Edward Hines had an idea. What if we painted a line down the middle of the road?

Until then, cars shared unmarked roads, which was... let's say chaotic. Inspired by that milky mess, Hines proposed painting a stripe to separate lanes. It caught on fast.

Today, road striping is standard across the globe, saving lives with every clearly marked lane.

A drippy truck. A sharp eye. A world of safer driving.

Sometimes it's the messes on the road that make them better.

99. The Pet Rock: Genius or Giant Joke? (1975)

In the 1970s, Gary Dahl joked about the perfect low-maintenance pet – a rock. No walks, no mess, no vet bills.

As a gag, he boxed smooth stones in straw-filled cartons with care instructions. People couldn't resist. He sold over a million Pet Rocks in just a few months.

It was part prank, part marketing magic, and a total pop culture sensation.

No batteries, no brains, just a stone and a very good idea.

From silly joke to million-dollar toy, the Pet Rock proves even the weirdest ideas can rock.

100. The Slinky Dog: Spring Into Toy History (1952)

After the original Slinky took over stairs and toy stores, inventor Richard James's wife, Betty, saw even more potential. What if it had a face? A tail? A wagging springy body?

Thus, the Slinky Dog was born – a mashup of physics and puppy.

It wagged, wobbled, and became one of the most beloved spinoffs of all time, eventually earning a starring role in *Toy Story*.

From stair-descending spring to adorable canine companion, the Slinky Dog proves that one invention can keep on bouncing... with a little imagination.

101. Paperclips: A Bend That Stuck (1899)

Norwegian inventor Johan Vaaler was trying to design a fastener that didn't need glue, string, or punching holes in paper. He bent a piece of wire into loops and curves, and accidentally created the **paperclip**.

At first, no one was impressed. It wasn't even patented in some countries because people thought, "It's just bent wire." But then office workers started using it anyway – and *loved* it.

It held papers together without damage, it didn't jam machines, and it could even unlock a jammed drawer if you were desperate (or sneaky).

Today, billions of them are made every year. And Johan? He became a national hero in Norway, for inventing something *mildly useful* in a major way.

From wire twist to worldwide desk domination, the paperclip proves that not all heroes wear capes, some wear... office supplies.

Did You Know? (Bonus Fun Facts)

1. Bubble Wrap was once used as greenhouse insulation.

Before it became a packaging pop-star, bubble wrap was tested as a way to help plants stay warm in cold weather. It *sort of* worked... but protecting fragile boxes turned out to be a lot less soggy.

2. The colour blue used to be more valuable than gold.

Ultramarine, made from crushed lapis lazuli, was once so rare and pricey that artists saved it for the robes of royalty and religious figures. Today, you can find it in crayons... and bathroom tiles.

3. The modern flush toilet was invented... then forgotten.

Sir John Harington (godson of Queen Elizabeth I) built a flushing toilet in 1596. No one cared. It took over 200 years and a guy named Thomas Crapper (yes, really) to popularize the idea.

4. Leonardo da Vinci sketched a working helicopter... in 1485!

His design, called an "aerial screw," never flew, but it looked a lot like modern helicopter blades. He was a few centuries early—and just a little short on engines.

5. Broccoli is man-made.

That's right! Ancient farmers bred wild cabbage plants over generations to create broccoli. Same goes for cauliflower, Brussels sprouts, and kale. Basically, your entire veggie drawer is a human invention.

6. Chocolate chip cookies were invented by accident.

Ruth Graves Wakefield ran out of baker's chocolate while making biscuits at her inn in 1938. She broke up a bar of semi-sweet chocolate instead, thinking it would melt evenly. It didn't – and the very first chocolate chip cookies were born.

7. Louis Pasteur made a major discovery on a chilly windowsill.

He once left a salt solution overnight, and the cold caused strange crystals to form. They revealed that molecules can be "left-handed" or "right-handed" – a tiny twist that became a huge moment in chemistry.

8. Ice-cream sandwiches began as a sticky solution.

A New York street vendor in 1899 squished a scoop of ice cream between two thin wafers to stop it sliding off the cone and onto the pavement. The idea caught on instantly – and the ice-cream sandwich was born.

9. Potatoes can power clocks!

Scientists in 1983 found that the acid inside a potato could conduct electricity well enough to run a digital clock. It wasn't quite lightning in a spud, but it proved lunch can be shockingly clever.

10. Glitter lamps were a sparkly slip-up.

A factory worker accidentally added shiny confetti to the wax mixture used in lava lamps. Instead of a disaster, it created a glittery, groovy new trend that shimmered through the 1970s.

Which Accidental Invention Are YOU?

Take this totally unscientific, completely ridiculous quiz to find out!

1. What's your favourite way to spend an afternoon?

A. Building weird stuff out of junk

B. Eating snacks

C. Daydreaming big ideas

D. Watching things explode (safely!)

2. What's your dream job?

A. Mad scientist

B. Dessert tester

C. Toy inventor

D. Secret agent

3. What's your biggest strength?

A. Curiosity

B. Creativity

C. Confidence

D. Chaos (with a side of charm)

4. Your friends describe you as?

A. Inventive

B. Hilarious

C. Slightly mysterious

D. Totally unpredictable

If you got:

Mostly A's: You're like Velcro—inventive, practical, and always sticking around.

Mostly B's: You're Popsicles—chill, sweet, and loved by everyone.

Mostly C's: You're X-rays—you see right through the surface and get to the good stuff.

Mostly D's: You're Silly String—wild, unpredictable, and *way* more fun than expected.

That's a Wrap! (Well, an Accidental One...)

You've just journeyed through 101 of the weirdest, wackiest, "wait, what?!" moments in invention history. Some were messy. Some were stinky. One involved cheese curdling in an old goat stomach (eww).

But *all of them* prove something amazing: you don't have to be perfect to change the world.

So go ahead, make mistakes. Tinker, trip, spill, doodle, and daydream. You never know what brilliant accident is just around the corner.

Who knows? The next big invention might come from **YOUR** next "Oops!"

Want Even More Brilliant Blunders?

You've just read 101 real-life oopsies that changed the world...
But guess what? We're not done yet.

There were a few weird, wild, and totally true discoveries that *didn't* make it into the book. (We ran out of room... or maybe we spilled ink on the list. Oops.)

Want to see them?
Get your printable extras pack:
10 Totally Bonkers Facts That Didn't Make the Book – A Printable Treehouse-Certified Reading Certificate – A Brain-Busting Brilliant Blunders Quiz – "Spot the Fake!" Fact Game – A Letter from me, T J Harvey!

Scan the QR Code at the end of this section or find it at: https://tinyurl.com/BrilliantBlundersBonus

Still giggling? You might also enjoy more books from T J Harvey!

Would You Rather? Gross, Silly, and Totally Bonkers!

Packed with more than 500 hilarious questions, this book sparks imagination and laughter for kids and families alike.

Inside you'll face wild choices such as:

- Would you rather have spaghetti for hair or hiccup bubbles every time you laugh?

- Would you rather eat a doughnut filled with slime or an ice cream made of broccoli?

- Would you rather talk like a robot for a day or bounce everywhere like a kangaroo?

You'll also discover:

- Bonkers Facts – Real-life weirdness that proves truth is stranger (and funnier) than fiction!

- Make Your Own Would You Rather? – Create your own outrageously funny questions!

- Totally Bonkers Bingo – Tick off your weirdest wins and see who gets five in a row.

- Bonkers Fact Challenge – Can you guess the answers to some totally bonkers facts?

- Gross Out Hall of Fame – Nominate your funniest "Eww!" moments and crown the champion of gross.

- Certificate of Bonkers Bravery – Earn your title as the ultimate Gross-Out Guru!

Search for **Would You Rather? Gross, Silly, and Totally Bonkers!** on Amazon, or scan the code at the end of this section.

Love Colouring?

Meet Some Funny Animals With Attitude!

A bold-outline colouring adventure full of **silly animal characters, short stories, and fun facts.**

Perfect for kids, teens, and adults who love creativity, relaxation, and giggles.

Inside you'll meet:

- A guinea pig magician who pulls carrots out of his hat.

- A koala explorer with a backpack full of snacks and big ideas.

- A chipmunk who plays the piano like a tiny concert superstar.

- A squirrel inventor whose Nut O Matic 3000 keeps firing acorns like popcorn.

- A sloth superhero in a cape, saving the day at super slow speed.

- A fish who guards the Great Undersea Treasure Chest.

- A rooster rocking out on a bass guitar.

- A bull who zooms around on roller skates, to the beat of his *moo-sic!*

With **clean, bold outlines,** it's suitable for young colourers and adults who enjoy stress-free, fun pages.

Psst! The QR codes for all your bonus extras and other books are waiting on the next page – ready to jump out and surprise you!

**Brilliant Blunders &
Fortunate Flops
Review**

Would You Rather

Brilliant Blunders
Bonus Content

**Funny Animals
with Attitude
Colouring Book**

We Want to Hear from You!

Did this book make you laugh? Learn something weird?

Gross out your little brother or sister, or even your parents & grandparents?

If you had fun reading Brilliant Blunders & Fortunate Flops, we'd love it if you left a quick review!

Reviews help other curious readers (and future accidental geniuses!) discover the book. Plus, it lets us know which stories made you say "Whoa!" and which ones made you snort juice out your nose.

Just a sentence or two is enough. Leave your review wherever you bought the book (there's a QR code on the previous page), or just tell a friend who loves weird facts and waffles.

Thanks a million for reading, and remember: the next great invention might just start with an "Oops!"

About the Author

T J Harvey once accidentally set off a glitter bomb while trying to open a birthday card, which might explain her obsession with happy accidents. She's a big fan of history, science, snacks, and silly stories, and sometimes writes all four at once. She lives in an English forest with a cat who thinks he's an inventor, and drinks way too much chocolate milkshake while writing things like this.

Your Notes, Doodles & Brilliant Mistakes

These next pages are yours. Draw something wild. Write down your best ideas. Invent something no one's ever heard of. Or just scribble and see what happens!

(Fun Fact: Thomas Edison filled over 3,000 notebooks during his career. You only need one to get started!)

Your Notes, Doodles & Brilliant Mistakes

Printed in Dunstable, United Kingdom